Michael Pedersen (b. 1984) is a poet, playwright and animateur with an electric reputation on the performance circuit and a prolific precedent of collaborations, having teamed up with some of the UK's top musicians, film-makers and artists. His inaugural chapbook *Part-Truths* (Koo Press) was a Callum MacDonald Memorial Award finalist; its sequel *The Basic Algebra of Buttering Bread* (Windfall Books) received flocks of reviewer plaudits. *Play with Me* is his (much anticipated) first full-length collection. Michael is co-founder and circus master at Neu! Reekie! – now one of the country's most formidable literary nights and DIY record labels – and a key creative within Dream Tower Productions. He's also the lyricist for cult band Jesus, Baby! and has written short plays for various troupes including the National Theatre of Scotland

http://www.facebook.com/neureekie
@NeuReekie
neureekie@hotmail.co.uk

Play with Me

Michael Pedersen

Polygon

First published in Great Britain in 2013 by Polygon,
an imprint of Birlinn Ltd,
West Newington House
10 Newington Road
Edinburgh
EH9 1QS

www.polygonbooks.co.uk

ISBN 978 1 84697 260 7

British Library Cataloguing-in-Publication Data
A catalogue record for this book is available on request
from the British Library.

Typeset by Koinonia, Bury, Lancashire
Printed and bound by Bell & Bain Ltd, Glasgow

Contents

III

IV

Acknowledgements

Some of these poems have been published in:

Gutter; *Northwards Now*; *Markings*; *Streetcake*; *Popshot*; *New Linear Perspectives*; *The Leither*; *nth position*; *Sentinel*; *One Night Stanza*; *etcetera*; *ink, sweat and tears*; *poet and geek*; *The Journal*; *3:AM Magazine*; *The Delinquent*; *anything anymore anywhere*; *The Poetry Kit*; *Read This Magazine*; *Reach Poetry*; *The Skinny*; *Part-Truths* (Koo Press) and *The Basic Algebra of Buttering Bread* (Windfall Books).

With thanks to those who helped along the way:

Ma and Pa; Carla Easton; Bréon George Ridell; Bill Ryder-Jones; KWD; Tom Bryan; Jonathan Freemantle; Kevin Williamson; Jesus, Baby! and Neu! Reekie!

And a mighty fond thanks to that over-worked editor o' mine, Gerry Cambridge.

I

Colmar

is a matrix of criss-cross canals, *capitale des vins d'Alsace*,
where, at thirteen, on the school French exchange,
        I met Elodie Mullan.
All summer, would insist on *cwassonts,* slurp *expresso*
and harshly defame Scotland;

for I knew nothing of our propinquity to the Rhine
or Vosges Mountains, only that Elodie lived a stone's throw
away, and with craned neck out the attic window
I could see her *boodwhar*, where there *must* have been
frequent episodes of nakedness.

Our moments were few: sat side by side on a boat tour;
locked hands walking through a rusting vineyard; were
dancing partners for three songs, linked
together like salted pretzels.

A photograph of us, in partial embrace, reveals Elodie,
alluring as Julie Delpy, me in a Scotland strip
with peroxide-blond hair. The sky, like the shirt,
ultramarine, and me blushing *rouge* from little-boy syndrome.

I used to dream of returning a celebrity,
with histrionics and extravagance. It would have been
horrendous: white limo, champagne, skunk, one-liners –
a scene from a tawdry hip-hop video.

Nowadays, I'd explain how a poem is like a bomb,
a bomb like a poem; assembled correctly, both
explode, they don't arrive, become
instantly important – as she did and could again.

RIP Porty High School

Edinburgh

From Europe's Mr Big Banana –
eight floors high, a thousand-
yard stare – to impending
Armageddon: the tower
block *will* topple. Its forty-
million-pound relocation
more a space-age
mutation; plans for portals
and pools leave old wifies
muttering
It's the parliament
aw over again.

Though bricks may fall
contradiction is immortal:
fluorescent *was* best for blending in,
and that *is* the popular crowd
strutting down the corridor
like Bojangles, on the balls
of their feet. Just ask
our notable alumni: Gail
Porter – TV presenter; Kenny
Anderson – boxer; James
Carlin – gangster.

The explosion is sure-fire
to muster a crowd:
bullied boys turning out
in thousands, who,

despite the salary, are
still clamouring
for comeuppance;
those that never got laid
resurface clutching hands
of svelte Thai brides,
pretending, now,
to like the *fitbaw*; others emerge
clasping books
of Collected Poems,
their names on the spine.

Midnight Cowboys

It's in the twilight hours
a father wakes his son –
Come on boy, we're off
to fetch a star. First

booted, then belted,
they set off, hand in hand,
pink on paler pink; scrambling
over scree, scaling

the frosted hills:
UP UP and UP – to where
galleries of brilliant bulbs
dangle like decorations

over a broody firmament.
But Pa, says the boy,
they're far too high for ropes
or slings, and we being poor

have only that. The father,
curtailing this lament, begins
to unravel a slice of sausage-
rolled rawhide. *Our month*

of Mondays just ended,
I've traded the ass for a fetcher.
Naked, under night's
open jaws, he brandishes a rifle;

its glistening resplendence rivals
any star. *These crosshairs*
will keep our eyes light
and bellies full for many seasons.

We'll pluck a star from the ether
like a thistle from the cairns.
It'll live in the barn
now the ass is gone!

Just seconds later bullets blast
– missed – missed – MISSED –
more and more kamikaze
into night.

Until . . . *You hit it Pa*, the boy carols,
in a voice that climbs the sky. Rapture,
as the biggest,
brightest bulb,

in sonic ascension, ziplines
through the dark. Both mouths
stretched
into O-shaped awe.

Nothing biblical about it, son,
but weren't that divine?
Perhaps best leave 'em be?
To which the boy replies nothing

more than a hushed *yeahhhhhh*,
and they amble homewards,
richer for not knowing
their chances of lassoing

the pearlescent package
were strictly chimerical;
for such beauties are screwed in
tight, falling only when ripe.

Laddie at Heart

At three-thirty I strode the buzzing
garden, entered an apricot door and stridently
announced an abduction. The illusive stranger:
he tried to take me – his leather bomber fastened
tight, puppies in the back of a beat-up Astra. Our

Bobbies on the job must have smelt a rat,
the story being nothing more than a sleazy replica
of the *Stranger Beware* tale they taught at school.
I made a statement, then marched a policeman
to a fictitious crime scene, barking boldly as I went.

By dropping in the odd nod of reverence –
I want to be a policeman when I grow up –
it panned out rather well. School signalled red alert,
Neighbourhood Watch was up in arms, and I
recounted details for tuckshop booty and lip kisses.

Conclusion: there's no better time for fame
than pre- the ego years. Silly to feign
a serious thing, but at ten – God knows what
I was thinking – it seemed a fair call. It's what I do
at twenty-five that gets my mother going.

Greenhouse Ganglands

Buttercups solicit ladybirds, pansies woo bees,
sparrows raid the strawberries. Mum sits
in peaceful observation, potting, then re-potting,
as scores of trespassers procreate and plunder.
Arthur's Seat and Other Peaks tower overhead –

behemoth bull seals, whiskers from a brawl.
The Ulster and the Paisley streets, a grassy
underskirt, hiked up, in floral theatre. Teeny tyrants
flee through thicket or burrow down when our
half-daft cat catapults

through the rhubarb. Bagged gooseberries
swirl, like wind spinners, on the back fence, a gift
from Mrs Fisher; her clothes pong of people
who spend too much time with boxes, but she's
a sorceress with fruit and sugar.

I parent my own pebbled plot, years four through seven:
radish, raspberries and Venus Flytraps,
which all die and I discover later were from Dobbies
(off the A7, Lasswade), not a far-off planet
of fiery infernos. Then came football stickers

and wrestling figures, to pioneer expeditions Mum
would often ambush, a scarf of spider plants gangling
round her neck; muddy paws like monster claws,
she chased the winds right out of me. This picture
was my teenage years' elixir.

With adulthood came predators far fiercer,
true ghouls, self-harm,
malignancies who too had monster claws,
but didn't flinch as beetles
crunched underfoot like celery.

Quitting Cheese

My discontent resides in Nottingham
along with some choice pubs
and a favourite day: The Tap, The Stage,
a trip to the park one afternoon
when everything was fresh; the clouds
shrugged out a little rain, the sun
huffed around them, our eyeballs
beamed – playful, light.

Picnicking was rife: foragers
ransacked the shrubbery, old relics
handed out hippy wisdom, we
feasted on each other, spinning
the conversational equivalent
of a roly-poly, living ubiquitously,
drinking a lot. I wasn't, *even once*,
an arsehole, just overused memory.

When we revisited Nottingham
the gaggle had gone and the winds
scraped against our bones;
we are a banquet folding
into a cheese cube too many,
bellyache, that fateful feeling
of having peaked too early.

Shapes of Every Size

With a *POW!* she sneezes
me out onto pub oak.
A myrtle emission
thumps, writhing
on the cider-steeped table.

A coaster is slapped atop
dense jelly, an upside-down
ashtray plopped on that.
It's sealed in, tight
as tinned beans, even
the pesky flies

won't get at it. It's done
and she marches
confidently out the bar –
a space shuttle, separating
between two solar systems.
That is the way to walk

when in love with your new shoes,
still blistered
by the old pair. Because
really missing someone,
like the python under my bed,
takes life by constriction.
We're each just little

pieces of puzzle trying
to find a fit, before we lose
our shape.

Feathers and Cream

This story is a secret
conglomerate of crumbs
smooshed into a carpet –
its sprawling sentiments,
like stretched bags,
have heat in them.

The mere mention of it
and your eyes are delicate seeds
creased in injury; language jolts,
suddenly fragile as dried leaves;
his palm prints illuminate
negatives of hugs from laps
of care. You share with me
your father:
attributes, ailments, quips
from games played, showcasing
a harvest of treasures
from his trips

abroad. Trust our peers
when things are grim
to release a gas of noxious rumour:
that a father's body went out
with bottles to meet the morning bread,
tipped from skip to local dump,
where metallic, apocalyptic jaws
minced through his brittle bones. In fact,
it was a stroke at home
that caused your earth to crumble.

For years it's had you hacking
at your arms, chucking up
the stomach's fiery soup – vitreous,
bludgeoned, rent,
a book spine-stripped.

So if you want
to be fourteen forever –
paused in fairytale parlours
on the eve of catastrophe,
pursed in ignorance,
hopeless, desperate but perfectly
beautiful – I'll be fourteen too.
And if you want to talk late
into night in solid circles
down to the indestructible
ashes of words clamped shut
like little fists, then
I'm talking too.

Owen

Reilly, deepest dreamer, sleeping
in the bedroom, brink pink
and handsome: a thousand
broken pieces, long black locks
like dirty cat tails, little feet
bouncing. How

he rests this way is beyond me
for whom night comes in chapters –
nods, intruded upon by light
turned tangerine
on clumpy floorboards. Soon

he's up,
straight for the rolling tobacco,
lungs like power stations,
a stormy cough.

Mornings spent tiptoeing
around resting Reilly
to the swirl of damaged vinyl
are among the prime-cut memories.
Nowadays, we're out of sorts –
though I still visit
the pictures, smiling, framing favourite
words through wine-stained lips.

We've both, I'm sure, said it out loud
(an aberration in a busy station):

I miss you,
afterwards feeling sheepish and exposed.

It seems his crooked teeth,
this crooked tale,
weren't quite as unsightly as first
I thought. Stories behind
scratches in wood.

CJ Easton

When each part of you flutes out
like the voiced pipes
of some elaborate organ,
you're not a thing grown thin –
that puny frame, its bag of bones
in winsome skin, will coruscate
and carousel.

Such a shift: where settled nights
in Carluke are suddenly prized,
more lauded than both
sides of America, than French
fables where, in chateaux, wine
is quaffed and laughter puffs
like excitable bonfires.

The crux of it: I was prickly
for you to know, a crafty seadog,
boasting admirations over aptitudes
for the stars – more troublesome
than torpid, louder when numb.
Imagine having missed this.

But things got back on course;
I outran night's galactic mischief,[1] balanced
out the receipts of my recklessness[2]
and in a divinely timed,
thrilling plumage YOU RE-ARRIVED.

1 Krakens stalking the ship, meteors circling your shadows.
2 The addled, smelted, hazy and heavy.

It's like when a car radio loses frequency
spilling down a deep fissure,
then, just as you forget about the music,
it bursts back, chirruping
a favourite song.

As pylons streak the sky
a ferocious sun sets over Glasgow,
bleeding, looking almost African,
it's *now* it could be true –
we're not so different you and I.[3]

3 (i) a (topsy-turvy) smile; (ii) little soldiers in the voice; (iii) pockets full
of cherry bombs.

Manchester John

Drips from leaky roofs.
Kids paw mangled movie mags;
their thumbed reviews of *Men in Black,*
Titanic, a sequel to *Jurassic Park*
are this ward's longest residents.

Slopped atop iron, you're
still and sere, rotting – a forgotten
banana. I tell the nurses *he's only*
twenty-two and what a hoot we had,
four of us, one bedroom, run-down
hotel on Corporation Street.

Bold and brazen, I wouldn't have it
any other way, but this is the third
overdose – things change
or you die. My tongue's trapped,
just like the oxygen bubbles they
think made it to your brain;
'Hypoxic Injury' sounds unreal
until crassly put,
re-labelled: cabbaged, crippled. Besides,
medical diction fails to touch
on the warm tingling bliss of horse
trotting up the arm – feels
better than they'd have you think.
Right, John boy?

So now you're Zimmer-framed,
shuffling as if you walked
on constant snow, feet throbbing
like frozen hands dunked in boiling water.

Pain's easier, it's
the emotional burdens of being
an ambulance hitchhiker
that *really* get you down. Namely,
the shame as a family
toss spiky words around
when drunk at get-togethers.

I leave the hospital and you
bleeping like a dying smoke detector.
Count the number of *sorry*s
that I owe you and you owe me
and we owe other people
until it all goes dizzy.

The Raven by My Writing Desk

Around us ravens loiter,
loom, crooked beaks
heaved open; cautel crafts
season in stern, sooty eyes,
black tongues ooze like poisonous slugs –
medusa among the animals.

I keep my eyes on them,
you and the barbecue;
meat smoking, sun simmering
on your eyelids, head tilted
towards the sky; the ground
around is warm, we've shed our socks,
the wind is at my back.

Offering upon offering is made
to hook-face scavenger:
peppered steak, onion bap,
a single anchovy – it is
an unusual barbecue. Eventually
the birds leave, and we leave,
chasing a summit, seeking
its panoramic sapience
from the forecasting of voyages
to the surveying of swans.
In this moment, I feel all my bones.

Later, you cast the invisible fishing rod
(just the way I taught you);
I pretend to be a snared trout,
spluttering towards the bank;
a capped man in a beer garden
glimpses, laughs, but kindly;

his dog makes a fuss; there's sun on the river;
you call me an idiot; we *both*
think it is funny!

What I neglect to tell you,
on the way down, is that I have decided
my favourite language
is lippy Scots: the tessellations
your tongue, quite indelicately,
draws on mine; talk of holidays
and buying ice-cream have never carried
such a thrill. And did you know
my preferred method of transport
is procession: tin whistles, trumpeteers
and triangles – the full nine miles,
every bit of the band. That's how it felt
today to walk with you. So next time
I wield a conversational pickaxe
with mistimed velocity
or head off on a squint orbit,
bear in mind, I probably ruined my night too;

                              the difference being

the ravens still stalk me,

hissing: *this*
                 one
                 knows
          a little more about death
                 than
                 he's
                 letting
          on.

II

Tom Buchan (1931–1995)

Tom wrote poems like fantastic pointing fingers
straight, strong and complex
as Glasgow; wrote

pulsing prose with pursed lips and served
verities caked in salt, bent rules
masterfully; captain

of a body well lived in –
chipped teeth, fractured bone, but enough
about his vessel.

Buchan brewed an eastern-western blend, so
like comets flew he spoke, in the heydays
and the greydays; moved

as a great touring caravan, compass pointing
north. Seven foot, they say, a strident mammoth,
a turtle-necked warrior.

It's possible we were, at some point, synched
in time and place, dragging our feet along the promenade
to Pittville Street, Portobello,

perhaps, too, shared insights on a story, spotted
the same flying kite, rogue gull, or submarine
surfacing in the Firth.

It bends wits, brooding over
what forces lobbied night sky to swallow
up a brightest star, and how

such verve came to plunge,
a rusty anchor,
into fierce waters.

Edinburgh Festival

From a spot of drizzle
starts belligerent rain:
it skelps make-up from faces,
smacks outfits with muck,
leaves audiences squelching

up and down craggy Edinburgh
gradients. Stormy weathers
besiege show-time
as a favour to the cabbie,
whose meter's on double.

I'm about first to arrive, already
there's fur on the throat
and yesterday's laughter
wrapped around my ribs
like soft stitches.

It's electrifying,
everyone gossiping, full fervour,
concocting *belles-lettres*
of those vying for five-star
pendants, crests or a tenner's
worth of airtime.

Come September, posters
in gutters turn to pulpy gruel,
tents recoil, marquees wince
and these flamboyant confabs
rapidly regress. I too flee

for Waverley; rather than
witness the emptying streets,
catch, in last glance,
a kilted drunk somersaulting
down the Mile – the way
our whole city does
at this time of year.

Cowgate Syvers

Stairwells natter in grey, blue and green
to snowmen, pigeons and passing
gangs of sparrows, yapping like Staffies
to every last bucketed mop.
Our antique Edinburgh tenements
bellow through the gales

and hails, cackling, as infants scurry
drenched to the bone, and traffic jams
fester – it's akin to how a passing boat
salutes another: a sturdy
honk on the horn and a wily
smile from the captain. The lighting:

everything from lanterns
to blinking candles battling drafts;
the smells exuded pack a pong –
musty, musky, wet and leathery.
But these fumes aren't noxious,
more like too much salt on supper.

I think of my favourite stairwells
as erudite elders: folded skins
and muckle beards they're twizzling
constantly, each a bard of handsome ken,
a hoarder of cadged chronicles.
These jovial giants stand

shoulder to shoulder with Gulliver and
my granddad. As for the rats,
gremlins and even more sinister
goings-on they host . . . well, we can't
all choose who comes to visit,
or at what hour they call.

With Divine Ovation

As a resident of Doonbrae,
she enjoyed the acreage and courtesies
of the artistes' benevolent fund,
a sixty-four-fold companionship, reciting
Shakespeare in the nightly cabaret
alongside other occupants, the jaunted
pastiche of their loyal visitants.

Colin, a fan first and nurse after,
made an impromptu stop
upon noticing her missed appointment
with Earl Grey and buttered
crumpets – there lay Eloise,
decubitus, stiff, dead.

A more courtly passing
you couldn't have asked for, not
tethered by wires nor sprawled
across iron, like pets on vets' tables,
but elegant, serene.

Colin shut the door,
lifted the rejected analgesia
 – morphine, a syringe pump –
and self-administered the full 15 mls;
on closing her eyes, mouthed
Bravo Eloise, taking his seat
for the encore.

Battle Cruisers

The twelve-pint team is fingernails fae fighting,
flinging fists like kids cast conkers. Cammy
and some gomper reach a deadlock
over fripperies: postcodes, a naff offside call.

He doesn't jump in, heid first, but trumpets
around like a bolshie rooster; six
disciples, hands unleashed, thump lumps
out of their floor-bound foes.

These dolts aren't a tight allegiance,
nor steadfast, just avoiding being strung up
for *pussying oot*. Saturday's rendition
of the foray occurs in cinematic stages:

trawling reels of metaphoric negatives, each
narrator freeze-frames his striking point.
Then it's off to The Rush – one last lecherous
expedition before sunrise. The place is a pit,

full of roistering lads and discount floosies.
Gordon wavers, chews over checking out,
when a cab pulls up like the moon: a beacon
of bright light and queer passage. He dives in,

barks out, *I'm awf, skint eh! Catch you guys
the morra for the draw*. Not quite an ethical
turn turtle, but there was real risk of a ribbing,
and he *did* tip the driver.

Heredity

Like his faither afore him,
ma faither kicked fuck oot ma maither,
ma maither battered us bairns –
me, I've ameliorated, I shower ma bird
wi savvy profanities, nae honds –
well, *just that once!*

And it shows, we noo live
in them posh hooses, clobbering
only the cat.
Mind you, nane of us drink thegether,
except, of course, at Christmas.

Jobseeker

On a June morning, sodden
and weepy, I came back
to the broo:

its accordion of tones
and teeth, the wild eyes
of hirsute residents.

Like a marsupial conceals
a cub, I cradle a book
of Armitage's poems,

weaving through words
as electronic Job Points
gesture like madmen –

a few clicks and they know *exactly* how much
trouble you're in.
Most of us pretend
we don't have to be
here, delivering a haughty hymn
of honeyed triumphs.

Midway through the poem
'Man with a Golf Ball Heart',
I'm accosted by Neil: his thinning

silver hair and evocative paunch
cast a hostile shadow.
Come right this way, Mr Pedersen.

We meet with a collective pinkness,
his tongue a ticking indicator,
my words skidding tyres

racing through every ailment
neither of us have. The day
had been a diagram, until:

Is there anyone under your care
or who cares for you, on a full-time
or part-time basis?

At this point I crumble.
Neil has broken me.
Would I be here if there was?

When I Fell in the Bog

The rest take taxis home;
I shrink out of sight
like a maniac, thrashing
through the long grasses,
parting carnivals of geese.
It took years of walking
this park to conquer
every precipice – a feat
the trees and I alone
dare flaunt, invincible as little lads
on high shoulders,
fire in their loose toes.

Rolling, then climbing,
I stumble at the sight
of a stag end-up in thick bog –
quicksand, we used to call it.
My chest, though locked,
gasps in laughter, fists full,
adulating. I remember a girl
fell in here and died.

Had it not been for a branch
and a mighty tug
I'd have done the same. Funny thing –
when it seemed I was going under,
my body relaxed, as if to say,
Tough break, but be glad
you're not smouldering
over the dailies.

Surprisingly Zen,
this almost dying; more like
being born.

In Marrakesh

Dawn's seeping inks
spaghetti into alleyways,
bright colours tug the eyes –
pixellated, red frays furthest.
If we'd stood a chance
of navigating through this place
it was slim, and slimming;
the kids knew it,
cajoling, biding time,
waiting to make a mockery
of us piggy visitors. Despite
my stubborn stances,
they've got us flummoxed,
grinding to a halt down a sandy
path like a narrowing stream.
It's into the pocket
for safe passage
to the souks, where
                    hands thrust out like spears,
            reaching for futures
they'll never hold, where ragged
fingers arrow at our arms
and nip the skin, as if to herd cattle.

A buffet of smells
sates the air, the scarab
blue of the sky turns tack
to treasure, tea cools on slabs.
I'm part of a chorus synched in barter –
for silvers sprayed with sand
on spliced wicker – there is no

impasse on price, just eagle
high, improvised or
me being impolite. He looks at us,
the merchant, sipping Coca-Cola,
stepping beyond his shadow,
reaching upwards
as if to gesture, *It's easy,*
pay a little more, there's always
that simple answer.

III

Newscast

Siem Reap is stitched together
with huts and hovels, electrical wires
and bent barbed fencing.

Each day begins to the oily trigger
of a moto-bike ignition, post-porridge,
pre- first garish sales pitch.

'Want to walk' flummoxes tuk-tuk
operators flanked by a bride.
Their red roads come

without a welcome,
quickly clot when damp,
clump, bubble and cook in heat,

forceful butchers tenderising meat.
Bees are bigger, beer is cheaper,
the coins have absconded for China,

the poor paper scuffed and over-worked,
like beloved old sneakers. Evening
conducts its own incongruous symphony,

fickle as the habits of fish; and though
I end bug-bitten, perspiring wildly, taken
for a mug and sometimes lonely,

I am happy in this wooden house, reading
a backlog of texts from a brimful list,
thousands of miles from all your news.

Justice Locale

It's on Sivatha Boulevard, Siem Reap,
where this speeding 4x4
ploughs down a Khmer kid –
his body catapults. Colours
crammed into a taut frame
spill, like berry punch, out
the ears and eyes and nose;
he's brown bread, dead weight,
ribs in double helix. A flurry of fumes,
then *putt putt putt* as furious
exhausts power off in pursuit.

Umpteen scooters skirt towards
the ostentatious chariot,
which veers from the road,
walloping a tiger tree.

A man is wrenched out, torn
from vehicle like stuffing
from a teddy bear. Korean:
Cambodia's Jew – 'not local'
would have been enough.
A seventy-strong siege
of swipes and stamps
leave him writhing,
a crushed worm
on the concrete slabs.

Late light sinks into the river,
fogs and culprits flee,
night unfurls, swiftly.

From the opposite bank I've time
to note caramel chinos caked in dust
and blood, his eyes
embers with the power
to come back from the dead,
if the right wind blew on them.

Arching Eyebrows and a Chalked Door

X marks the spot of visceral malevolence:
cracked lips, thin as slits on wrists, converge
like tyre tracks. Sweat pours past blemish
and blister, words rock back and forth,
kids on swings. This is a man condemned:
a gravy-blooded, Xed, hexed body filled with AIDS.
As with all commanders of devilry, he purveys
vicious charms: many men, fond of fame,
have followed him to battle; each *battue*

comes cloaked as *coup d'état*. Jean:
an Algerian abdicator, a French defamer,
an aficionado of wartime suffering –
how at home he felt, hiding out in Nam, flogging
filth to US soldiers. Under stolen stars
they sparked Lucky Strikes and staked out
claims for infinity. Now on sojourn, in Cambodia,
he's bragging to strangers, about harm,
necessity, seeing things through.

Assumes each too wasted to collect quotes,
tap scales or severities, too scared to repeat
the rendezvous. Regrets? Only misfortune:
I'll never see my son grow old. I'm withered,
dying because of heroin. Cut loose by two countries,
pariah to both cultures. Had I been on spirits
I'd have piped up and said it: *If I ever*
meet your son, I'll tell him his dad was a monster
who called Bob Dylan an asshole.

Hello. I am Cambodia

who wakes every morning,
in a brilliant mood, as caskets
of mischievous light scorch soil
into mottled polka dots.

My Cardamom Mountains,
fluffy as cats, thatch mossy quilts
over Pol Pot's bones.
Among markets
fruits conspire
like multicoloured aliens,
and bumblebee catfish, having
outrun river wolves,
find themselves bucketed
in half-dollar kilos.

Happy days. A new age
of lionising afternoons,
blithesome eavesdropping:
rosy guests swap
shibboleths over
piña colada and sugared cherries.

I've not forgotten
the old regime, not yielded
a single search for solace.
My monuments await
restoration, half my population
is children, we play together,
though I'm elder, ancient,
abstaining from scratching
as wounds cicatrise.
I've not forgotten the old regime,
I just wear it well.

Postcard Home

Whiteskin teaches children:
modals, syntax, intonation;
learning *not* to be so

fatalistic, so serious
for home; how to pay the family
thanks. With friends

will practise market origami:
seeding guava, peeling star-fruit,
and I bought a bicycle –

its yellow frame with wire basket
is sure to make you laugh.

BoomTown

She is a tall bright Sihanoukville noon,
dress hiked up to the pelvis, sun thumping
down on the commotion: a sandy kid has pulled
an unexploded bomb from a sack of spoiled greens.
It gleams beastly, bright as any US import;
the throng of the crowd like a lit match.
Probably a dud, but if it had gone off, we all
like to think we'd have moved a little quicker.

At the whites full of worry, Khmers giggle:
insouciance and awe, a dozen smiling faces
grin straight back – and that's before dust-
downs or touch-ups. We make an exchange slap bang
in the middle of a high street, 3,000 riel to hold it,
but worth every sweating note. As if cradling
an animal, something stirs inside my gut,
disturbs the sticky rice and stomach worms.

You arrive this same day with a bang
of a different sort, by Kang Ken airstrip,
amidst landing lights and neon fuzz,
grandiose – as only a foreigner could
in this port city. Boats bring you here,
alongside nameless infants and trade narcotics –
that way you're not salting the wounds
of Mother Cambodia. Narith drops us

by *noisy dog* or *cockerel pen*; it's easier
than saying *King Gold Hotel*, for me,
who's trying to fit in. Though lovely even
at your most captious, it's a short walk

and you just wouldn't get it. In the same way
you won't go barefoot or cut through jungle fringes,
you curse philandering monks
buying dollar drinks for local ladies.

I tame your pique with trips to Victory
and Serendipity beach, rent us a *sunbrellas*, but
your thoughts are further off than home,
and the growl in my glare grates at the softness
of your skin. Three weeks of mating
and mutiny and I've aged a year. So
move on, sign your name on the sheet –
like bluebottle blood the ink turns sticky.

Ten nailless toes on a rickshaw driver
evoke one last whimper before you fly
back to London, to spring's unexploded bloom.
I stay here with this silent bomb;
me in the eastern hemisphere, you
in the West, me an alley cat,
slight sunburn all over, you
with eyes slant.

From the Right Bank

the left bank fans out
into sleek spines of sand;
drunk knees surrender
as if slipping off their bones.
Dusk sets differently, a stray
dog's pinched eyes
trail steam hissing
from a pot; barks
bound skywards, skidding
into darkness.

On the Reaper's left bank
lurks Fata Morgana: a landing
strip, zoned off for men
to don dainty frocks
and sequined skirts; icing
sugar-bright. By day

they're stick-up boys,
guidebook pundits
or the uncordially schooled,
by night a cavalcade
of sharp laughs, struts,
deliberated colour
where chintzy eruptions
of chatter and playful fondles hook
handsome man stumbling home.

As for wee Scotty, he'll prance by
pulverised; crumpling the quiet,
one night, takes hold
of her hand, limps

to the bank's edge and spurts
triumphantly
out into the current
like a rogue pup, as the moon, giddy,
gawks, from above.

No. 58, Slorkram, Siem Reap

This stilted house (of heavy heart) speaks
out in castigation of the card-counting
swindlers gambling by the river.

Ferny feet hide secrets buried deep
in the soil, down beneath the timber,
where, all earthy, only spiders stray.

Together we watch the sky like television
screens: lapis days turn back to black-
booted nights, but we natter on,

letting colours creep and silence settle
behind the shadows of shrubs –
think milk mixing into tea. Tonight

the ether eyeballs us, winds gallop
from tufts to yarns, settle in yawns –
a tell-tale sign to shamble off to bed.

Remember Michael (with a voice
brass as bells), *inside all bones are white
and souls are soft as ripened mango.*

*Of course. I won't forget it.
And tomorrow, can you tell me the story
of the Big City who lost his feathered hat?*

Network: Cambodia

Sunrise springs from behind dustbins,
pours through alleys, pounds down streets
like a terrible gang. We're in a town

fat from rumour, full of cavaliers
straying from their safe zone, each set
on becoming our local luminary, parenting

a legacy to ship westwards into the living rooms
of old schoolmates and ex-girlfriends.
They're bananas not to notice

Khmer cachet is strictly local currency
and the traveller to expatriate evolution
has a lot in common with invisible ink.

These fellows crave envy over talent
or kisses – it's like having a whole heap
of brooms without bristles. I'm busy

enjoying night: sheet feeds into my creases
like wax set around cheese, my belly
bubbles full of fish, bare walls

make for good thinking. How about the way
those kids played hop-scotch, tossing stones
overhead – a trick I never learned.

IV

X Marks the Spot

When we first met
you were too drunk to remember,
storing me (my looping arms,
cherry cheeks, trespassing
tongue) in your phone as lonely
Letter X. But I sort of dug

the anonymity – what's in a name
after all? As X, I'm Roman ten,
daunting, a variable – the nomad
of the alphabet; I'm raunchy
racy top-shelf triple X –
an emblem, not a word:

a superhero, of sorts.
The next day – by text –
my X is resurrected on your screen.
My message, too, will end
in X – a carnal bounty
for your pirate eyes.

Another meet, another kiss:
X morphs into Carla,
Carla, to an affectionate farrago:
Slugger, Muffley,
Toots, Moon-Pie.

We croon and cuddle,
bundling under your covers
and mine. Life was a sack
of strawberries, the future, jams
and spice. ALAS – I am
a SNOOP. Left alone I will

peruse your personals, burgle
your belongings; searching for
a bottle-opener
I stumble across your phone –
Come to MAMA. A professional
has an eye for it – whizzing past

amorous gunk, poetic prattle, like
a boxer skipping rope.
Let's get straight to the yolk:
this address book *has* grown
and where once was *my X*
there now is another!

A trophy letter, slumped
to a stamp of expiration,
no curlicues to mitigate its twin
crossing blades; X
the executioner; X a weapon
of infallible symmetry.

Times New Roman
doesn't beat around the bush:
my years under your cover,
once absolute, suddenly
a shoddy leasehold tenure.
Nothing else for it,

time to take the plunge:
CALLING X – the ringing phone
cackles out with wry
tintinnabulation.
A silken, exotic voice
answers, with perfect

tongue and intonation
Good eeeevening
. . . you're through
to The Thai Palace.
Please order by inserting the number
of the dish you desire.

Ahhhhhh finest of fortunes,
pangs of a different stock.
You do love me!
Me, your estate for life,
love to the X
year – *pur autre vie.*

Fever

It's like an oven in here: air cake-icing
sticky, steeped in sweat – best
place for it, above the covers, breasts

flat on the chest. Who'd have thought
skin rises like yeasty bread and the body
like a sun like helium like mist.

You breathe so lightly, purr, as if your lungs
are making music – notes soon toppled
by my demolition breath.

The room pulses, damp, bulbous; geckos
on walls balloon to the same primordial beats –
we've acknowledged this, the reptiles and I.

Their berry gaze understands hands touch hair,
joints creak, skin slips, all in reminder
we are capricious mammals, keepers

of uneasy conscience, like a spinning top
near stop. If we stay together, me tit to your tat,
vice-versa, I will never yell *Areeeba!* –

really mean it. You will never drop those sighs
into the sea. Unlike the sunflower
which arrives in annual bloom, these moments
come, then go, just the once.

Expired Treasure / Broken Bulbs

Among diggers, demolitions, dead pets,
wispy men strut with unfastened zippers, sucking
ice poles in the sun.

A ransacked leisure centre from my PE days,
now a womb for veteran glue sniffers
and gang initiations.

The Figgy Burn's cemented banks
exhibit expired treasure: mangled prams,
hijacked trolleys, 80s electronics;

the pubs have trade names: The Glass Blower
(vandalised to ribaldry),
Cobbler's Thumb, The Market Thief.

Inside each a landlord snarls, exposing teeth
like a string of broken seashells –
head honchos with first dibs

on the local munters. As for
the town beauty, she rehearses
her exodus nightly:

through dirty ocean eyes, pictures
life 'abroad'. Her note to read:
See you in hell (if you're lucky)!

Kisses, Wendy xXx

Hello Bréon, it's nice to meet you,

please ignore the scratches, I've
been browning in gutters,
amongst wet cigarettes and the last
flecks of Camden's lanceolate leaves.

As things stand faith is grubby,
sweet premise pale, the railings, too,
have lost their stockings – nowt
but dankness underneath.

I've noticed your stories don't involve
sticky risings, Senegalese dealers,
Lambeth car parks: I am
intrigued, but for fear

you'd think me mad (or
a poor secret-keeper), I snub
the amber suns which clockwork
through the firmament. For you,

too, blaze, thatching synergies,
talking of six continents
operating like organs. It took years
before I spoke about the stars:

blinking blinking, as night
rivers round them.
To which you replied *Ahhh,
the stars! I thought you'd never ask.*

Paris in Spring

After three days of heavy saucing,
I am in tatters, bowels barking
like a backfiring exhaust.

The Alexander Technique has failed
me, the bus is overcrowded,
this pie, this paper and I are damp,

I'm late. Even the book pages pound.
Let's see: despotic emperors,
tiny tombs, knotted lace, itchy cloth.

But just as pith can clean
the orange, the sun can scour
sky, traffic shift, the clock

fall back an hour. I flick the page;
we're now discussing
Paris in spring.

The End Was Colourful

and well articulated: smalt
blue – plashes – sap
green, spectrum orange.

You painted over our secret constellation.

The sky again
is a jumble-sale;
I'm pinballing, a pup
chasing anything
that moves. One last frightful time,
let's start over, each wink
an orbit.

The Day Is Dreich

and that's not the half of it;
tetchy rains puncture mist,
further steepen the wynd,
torrents bind borders
around sinking grounds.

A cagouled dog walker:
You must be mad! Wet arsed,
snacking beneath birches, having
overdone the condiments –
the bread, too, is dribbling.

The weather changes, spins
a revolution –
it's us who won't revisit
our starting point. We sit
down with the summit
like guests at a formal dinner,
gauche, uncomfortably dressed,
a little too close to each other.
I've been here before, every
implement imaginable
set upon the table, not a clue
which tool is best
for tackling this plateful.

Dead Skin and Stray Fingernails

I often sneak a peek at your old house
up Duddingston Grove, shift
from brisk stroll to bimble, and hover
on the corner.

The driveway is busy, the drapes
no longer droop – it'll be their dead
skin and stray fingernails
infused within the furniture. Meaty

aromas filter through the conifers –
a barbecue is underway:
midges fleeing spirals
of smoke, vim, *vino,* puffs

of laughter. All the tragedy this house
has seen – you think I'd celebrate their good
living and leave in peace.
But I want them out and you back

in, because we forgot to finish
our most important conversation.
So, for one last time, I slash the tyres
of their Nissan Skyline and, hopeful, head
for home.

Water Features

Your voice is a balloon, getting
further and further
away.

My smile, a child
saying *Look at me! Pay me
attention!*

Our likeness, water, was
why we came together;
to cascade and thrum,

trickle and splash – roving
torrents, river folk who young
and giddy rushed

their waterfall,
cutting too deep, too fast,
battering the banks

and sliding into earthy
separation – an ox-bow lake
divorced

from its ambitious river;
one of us running,
the other stilled.